sew simple squares

sew simple squares

More Than 25 Fearless Sewing Projects For Your Home

WATSON-GUPTILL PUBLICATIONS / NEW YORK

Kathy Peterson

PHOTOGRAPHY BY
Christopher Lincoln

Fabric pictured on pages 12, 13, 37, 51, 55, 61, 62, 66, 69, 76, 80, 82, 84, 92, 98, 100, and 104:
Fabric design © 2002 Waverly. Reprinted with permission. All rights reserved. Fabric used in illustrations courtesy of Waverly.

Fabric pictured on pages 90, 97, and 108:
Courtesy of Daisy Kingdom.

Senior Editor: Joy Aquilino
Project Editor: Anne McNamara
Designed by pink design, inc. (www.pinkdesigninc.com)
Graphic production by Hector Campbell
Text set in Bembo and Syntax

First published in 2003 by Watson-Guptill Publications,
a division of VNU Business Media, Inc.,
770 Broadway, New York, N.Y. 10003
www.watsonguptill.com

Library of Congress Control Number: 2002111272

ISBN 0-8230-4782-2

Manufactured in Malaysia

First printing, 2003

1 2 3 4 5 6 7 8 9/09 08 07 06 05 04 03

I would like to dedicate this book to my mom and dad, John and Lorraine Peterson, for sharing years of guidance and support. Their wonderful creative talents, love, and generosity are deeply cherished.

acknowledgements

In writing *Sew Simple Squares,* I asked for the help and support of several friends and companies to whom I owe much appreciation. It is with great thanks that I wish to acknowledge the following:

Husqvarna Viking Sewing Machines for making all of the home décor projects in this book so much fun to sew. Lucille J. Grippo from Waverly® Lifestyle Group and the folks at Daisy Kingdom for supplying me with many of the wonderful fabrics used in the projects. For all of the beautiful trims, I must thank TrimTex, Wrights®, Prym-Dritz, and JewelCraft. Special thanks to Fiskars® and Prym-Dritz for their wonderful lines of cutting and measuring tools, and to Fairfield Processing for all of the pillow forms, poly-fil, and batting products. Thanks also to Carolina Manufacturing for Hav-A-Hank bandannas, and to Coats and Clark for their terrific dual-duty all-purpose threads and embroidery floss. For the glue, thanks go to Diane Newman from Beacon Adhesives, and for the iron-on adhesives, thanks go to Therm-O-Web.

For sharing their beautiful homes, many thanks go to Betty Firing, Nina Tozzi, Julie Letender, and Michelle Sousa. I also wish to share my appreciation with photographer Chris Lincoln for making the shooting sessions fun and unforgettable. Hugs and kisses go to my husband Tom Knapp for his support and love during the five months of creating this book. And finally, much appreciation goes to my editor, Joy Aquilino, whom I admire and appreciate as a friend.

contents

preface

Who says a square is just a square? Not me! I see fabric squares as window treatments, bed, chair, and table covers—even comfy pillows! And you will too, when you discover how to transform simple squares of fabric into fast and easy home decorating projects.

Throughout my career as a designer, I have been blessed with the ability to look at an ordinary object and see a treasure-trove of creative ideas. I could never bear to part with fabric left over from craft and sewing projects, not knowing what my imagination might dream up for them. And fabric-finds, like bandannas and linen napkins, were the source of countless inspirations.

Although I learned how to sew at an early age, I grew to become just an "occasional sewer," using my little portable sewing machine only as needed. But lately I've rediscovered the ease and pleasure of sewing, and have found it to be a wonderful way to express myself creatively. In conceiving my designs, I always try to keep the process enjoyable and the end-result pleasing to the eye.

A square is more than just a scrap of fabric. Behind every square is the making of countless home decorating projects just waiting to be conceived.

Sew Simple Squares is meant to encourage the novice sewer to explore the pure joy and simplicity of sewing. To do this, each project in this book is based upon a simple fabric square. There are no patterns to pin down and no complicated sewing techniques or skills to master. I've kept the projects ultra-easy by taking you step-by-step from cutting the fabric into squares, layering and positioning the squares, and finishing with basic stitches and adhesives.

This book is filled with a wealth of wonderful home accents for your kitchen, dining room, bedroom, patio, or any other room of your house. Every page will encourage you to tap into and refine your personal style so you can add warmth to your home and create cozy interiors that you will enjoy and appreciate for years to come. So get ready to Sew Simple Squares!

chapter 1

Materials and Supplies

I'd like to start this chapter by taking the apprehension out of sewing. If you have never sewn or are a beginner, you will need first to familiarize yourself with a few essentials. Sewing can be fun as long as you have the right tools and materials available. Even something as basic as what sewing machine you use can make a big difference in your level of enjoyment.

choosing fabric

The most significant factor in the success of your project is the fabric chosen. Because of their stability and ease, I used cotton and cotton blend fabrics for most of the projects in this book. Cotton and cotton blends come in many forms, from corduroy to velvet, and are available in an endless variety of colors and prints. They stand up to repeated washings and can be treated to be waterproof and stain resistant, making them a good choice for items that will be heavily used. Linen is another attractive option for home furnishings. It is durable, versatile, and can be laundered and pressed.

Not only is the type and quality of fabric you purchase important, but also the pattern or print, texture, and color that you choose. Select a fabric that you love, as it will become an important part of your living space. Be sure it blends with your decorating scheme and fits the mood you want to convey.

When shopping, always try to view fabrics in natural daylight to get an accurate impression. If you plan to combine fabrics, lay them next to each other to observe their interplay.

Fabrics with directional patterns, such as toile, can be cut in various ways to frame and showcase the motifs. Determine how you would like to cut the fabric before purchasing, as additional yardage may be required.

FABRIC GLOSSARY

Before you begin to sew, familiarize yourself with some fabric "basics."

Bias: This runs diagonally or on a 45-degree angle from the grains of the fabric. Cut fabric on the bias for the greatest amount of stretch.

Face: The right side, or "attractive" side of the fabric.

Fiber: The basic material, either natural or manufactured, used to produce fabric.

Grain: This is the direction in which the fabric threads run. Grains of fabric run lengthwise parallel to the selvage, and crosswise between the selvage edges.

Selvage: This is the finished edge that runs along the side of a length of fabric and prevents raveling. It is usually woven tighter than the rest of the fabric, and often carries company information and/or color matching dots.

Warp: In woven fabric, this refers to the yarns that run lengthwise and are interwoven with the fill (weft) yarns.

Weft: In woven fabric, this refers to the filling yarns that run perpendicular to the warp yarns.

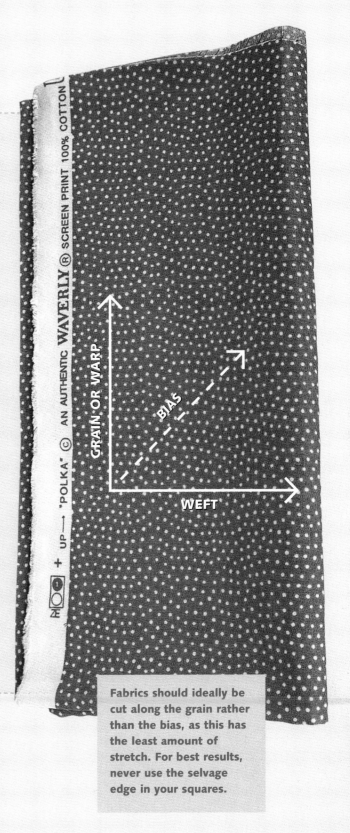

Fabrics should ideally be cut along the grain rather than the bias, as this has the least amount of stretch. For best results, never use the selvage edge in your squares.

choosing colors and prints

I've chosen and combined a wide variety of fabric prints and colors for the projects in this book. You can either adhere to the selections shown, or use them as inspiration for your own marvelous mixes.

Whether working with solids, prints, or a combination of both, let color be the unifying theme. Contrast colors for a dramatic look, or use similar colors for a harmonious effect. A simple method for coordinating fabrics is to pull a color from a print and build around it. Likewise, fabrics in matching colors but different textures often pair nicely.

When working with prints, take special note of the size or scale of the design. While a small-scale print may first appear to be the best choice for a little project, a larger print may also be effective, either trimmed down or used as a focal point.

If you plan on combining patterns, strive to achieve a visual balance. Couple a bold print with a smaller one, a floral with a stripe. When you select a combination of three fabrics, it's always safe to use a geometric, a floral, and a solid or small print.

If your fabrics appear a little dull, liven them up with a shot of black, white, or a vivid primary color. Soften a strong contrast with a neutral gray or beige. Most of all, I encourage you to feel free to experiment. Ultimately, the right combination is what looks and feels right to *you*.

Solid-colored fabrics are available in a broad spectrum of colors. Small prints read as solids from a distance. Tone-on-tone fabrics, like damask, also appear as solids, but with an added layer of texture and design.

Textured fabrics have nubs, ribs, tucks, or a nap. Nap fabrics, like chenille, velvet, and corduroy, have a fuzzy or downy surface. Working with a textured fabric can be challenging, so practice sewing a scrap piece of fabric before starting your project.

Geometrics consist of plaids, stripes, dots, and checks. Be sure to keep the lines straight when cutting and piecing plaids and stripes. Match designs like stripes and plaids at side seams for a polished finish.

Figural, scenic, or floral prints depict realistic settings or objects, such as flowers, people, and animals, in a natural manner. If a design has a predominant repetitive motif, center it on the front and back of your project whenever possible.

Fabrics with stylized designs have familiar shapes that are somewhat distorted and embellished, such as a tear-drop paisley, or recognizable patterns that are exaggerated or simplified. Abstract fabric designs have non-realistic shapes and patterns.

trims

Trims and beads are wonderful embellishments that can enhance your sewing projects. Ruffles, cording, pom-pom fringe, bullion fringe, gimp, ribbon, and an assortment of others are used in this book. Each has its own appeal and can be combined and used creatively for a variety of looks.

Trims can be inserted in seams or, as with rickrack and ribbon, applied over a seam or along a finished edge. Secure trim with fabric glue, fusible adhesive tape, or machine or hand stitching. Look for trim in your local craft or fabric store, or refer to the list of suppliers in the back of this book to find the nearest retailer. When shopping for trim, take a sample of your fabric along to match colors and textures.

Trims can make plain pillows appear posh. Try combining beads with ribbons, tassels with cording—whatever strikes your fancy.

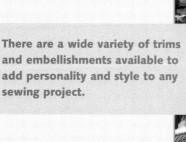

There are a wide variety of trims and embellishments available to add personality and style to any sewing project.

sewing machines

When it's time to buy a sewing machine, it's easy to get overwhelmed by all the decisions involved. Not only do you need to consider what kind of machine you want, but also what features and functions you need. To limit the selection, determine beforehand what kind of sewing you plan to do and how much money you can spend.

Before purchasing your machine, discuss the options with other sewers. Visit a reputable independent dealer and ask for advice. See if accessories are included (needles, bobbins, zipper foot) or if they can be bought easily. Ask about the buttonhole procedure. Depending on the machine, this process can range from one to five steps. Also ask how many decorative stitches are offered. For the projects in this book, you'll want a sewing machine that has decorative or embroidery stitching options.

I've chosen to sew with a computerized machine that allows me to embellish fabric with a wide variety of stitches, sew with ease, and complete each project in a reasonable amount of time. It has many special features, including a built-in disk drive for machine embroidery, a self-adjusting presser foot, and a large color touch-screen. There's even a thread cutter and a needle threader that makes changing threads a snap. This type of machine will surely expand your imagination and provide you with hours of sewing enjoyment.

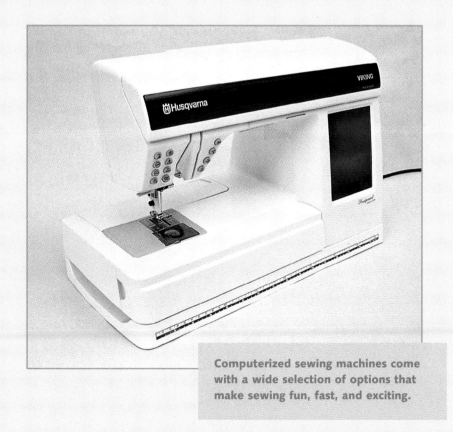

Computerized sewing machines come with a wide selection of options that make sewing fun, fast, and exciting.

measuring tools

Clear acrylic rulers are used for measuring and as a straightedge for rotary cutting. They have variable grids or sight lines for lining up fabric, and are available in different shapes and sizes. For the projects in this book, I used square acrylic rulers with ¼-inch or ⅛-inch grid marks. (If a square ruler is not available, substitute with a straightedge.) Start by purchasing several sizes of squares or the largest square available. Square rulers can be purchased at sewing and quilting stores.

A 60-inch tape measure and sewing gauge are sufficient for measuring the placement of the squares and seams in this book. Your cutting mat will also have a measuring grid. As the old saying goes, measure twice and cut once.

Clear acrylic rulers and mats are used for measuring and rotary cutting. Use a flexible tape measure to measure surfaces.

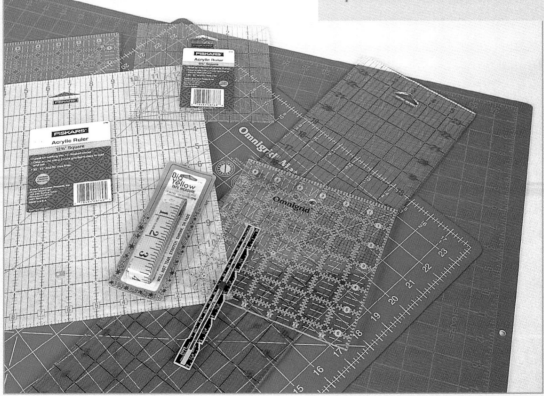

cutting tools

Rotary cutters come in a variety of sizes. The size you choose will depend on how many layers of fabric you wish to cut. For example, use a larger blade and cutter to cut several layers of fabric at once; use a smaller blade and cutter to cut a single layer of fabric. If a rotary cutter is not available, you can use scissors to cut the fabric squares. To reduce hand fatigue, look for scissors and rotary cutters that offer cushion contour grips and an easy-action spring that opens after each cut. (For safety, always close the blade to prevent finger cuts.)

Use a snipper or embroidery scissors to trim loose thread ends. Seam rippers have a sharp, curved edge used to rip seams open and remove stitches. There is a safety ball at the tip of the ripper to protect fabric.

CUTTING MATS

When you use a rotary cutter you must use a cutting mat. This is a protective cutting surface that can also be used as a measuring guide for fabric. When choosing a cutting mat, look for one that is self-healing with a grid. For the projects in this book, the mat should measure at least 17 by 23 inches. Always place mats on a hard, flat surface while cutting. Store mats flat to avoid warping, and keep them away from heat and direct sunlight. When working, vary where you cut on the mat. If you always cut in the same spot, that area will wear quickly.

batting, pillow forms, and fiberfill

Batting, pillow forms, and fiberfill are available in a variety of fibers, sizes, and lofts. (Loft refers to the thickness.) The fibers can range in part from 100 percent cotton to cotton blends, or polyester.

Pillow forms can be made from polyester fiberfill, pellets, or foam. If you prefer natural fillers, there are pillow forms stuffed with down and feathers, as well as woolen fleece. Foam forms are molded into shape and can sometimes be a little stiff. To soften a foam form, wrap it with a layer of batting before inserting it in your cover.

Fiberfill comes in a range of densities. Fiberfill pillow forms come in sizes ranging from 10 to 30 inches, in round, rectangular, square, and cylinder shapes, among others. Fiberfill pillows are graded either standard or superior. Superior forms have a greater loft and generally have fabric covers. Fiberfill is machine washable and allergy free. If you are making a pillow in a non-standard size, you can make your own pillow cover from muslin and stuff it with loose fiberfill.

Made in both cotton and polyester, batting is sold in sheets in crib, craft, king, queen, and twin sizes. In addition to stuffing bed covers and quilts, batting can be used to lightly pad surfaces and add softness to edges. It can be used effectively to cushion chair seats and backs. Use as many layers as desired and tack it in place so it won't shift.

Batting, pillow forms, and fiberfill add softness and support to home sewing projects.

threads, needles, and pins

Threads, needles, and pins are sewing essentials. Let your fabric guide your needle and thread selection.

Threads, needles, and pins are instrumental for successful home sewing. Always select threads in a thickness that suits the weight of the fabric. All-purpose cotton or cotton-wrapped polyester thread, rayon thread, and embroidery floss are used in this book. Generally, rayon threads are used for decorative or embroidery stitching. All-purpose cotton or cotton-wrapped threads can also be used for this type of stitching, but are more often used for general sewing. Embroidery floss can be used to embellish projects with decorative stitches or to tie-off a bedcover (see "Tying-Off," page 57). To keep the stitchwork subtle and discreet, choose threads in colors that match or complement the fabric.

Needles and pins come in a variety of sizes. As a rule of thumb, always use pins and needles that suit the weight of the fabric. I recommend using medium-length needles for hand sewing in sizes 7, 9, and 10 (the higher number indicates a finer needle). For beading, use a beading needle. For tying-off bed covers, use a large-eye embroidery needle.

Use straight pins to hold fabric layers together. Pins with large multi-colored heads are easy to see and handle. I like long pins with extra-sharp points for home décor projects. When sewing, place pins at a right angle to the seamline with the heads to the right of the presser foot. Large safety pins can be used for holding the layers of a bed cover together when tying-off or quilting.

adhesives

Using the right kind of adhesive is critical to the success of your project. I recommend using a quality fabric glue to adhere the trims shown in this book. Fabric glues dry flexible and clear. They form a permanent bond and can be used as an alternative to sewing. Fabric glues are washable, but are not recommended for dry-cleaning.

For larger surfaces, such as a fabric square, I recommend using a fusible adhesive. Fusible (or iron-on) adhesives work well adhering and stabilizing fabric squares, and they eliminate the need for pinning. Fusibles are available in sheets, as well as in tapes of various widths. They come in different adhesive strengths to suit different weights of fabric. Fusible tape can be used to apply trims and appliqués, and even for hemming. Paper-backed sheets of lightweight fusible adhesive will work best when making the projects in this book. (See "Using Fusibles," page 33 for application guidelines.)

Fabric glues are specially formulated to adhere to woven cloth. Use the glues to apply trims and fabric embellishments. Paper-backed fusible adhesives are fabulous for joining fabric layers.

miscellaneous supplies

A good iron and ironing surface are sewing essentials. Use a combination steam-dry iron with temperature control. Be aware of the type of fabric you are ironing and select the proper setting. When ironing, use a padded ironing board or folded towel as a protective surface.

Stabilizers should be used to add body and support to delicate and lightweight fabrics. However, in most cases, since you are using iron-on adhesives before sewing, a stabilizer may not be necessary. Like iron-on adhesives, fusible stabilizers are applied to the wrong side of the fabric before cutting.

If you cannot access a square acrylic ruler, use a fabric marker with a straightedge ruler to draw out your fabric squares. Fabric markers are designed to be easy to see and easy to remove. Use a disappearing fabric marker, which evaporates over time, or a water-soluble marker if you plan on washing the finished item. Probably the best all-around marker is tailor's chalk. Tailor's chalk comes in square and triangular shapes and in a variety of colors. The marks can be removed with a fabric eraser or brush. There are also chalk pencils available whose marks wash out and/or evaporate.

STOCKING UP

There is nothing as frustrating as having to interrupt your sewing to run out to replace some essential tool or notion. That's why it's always a good idea to stock up on basic supplies so you will never find yourself short-handed. Keep an eye out for sales and other bargains so you can get the most for your money. Collect buttons and threads in your favorite colors. If using novelty buttons, always purchase a few extra just in case one is lost. Keep a supply of replacement sewing machine needles, bobbins, and other often-used equipment. Purchase fusible web in 5 yard cuts to have sufficient amounts always readily available. Keep a spare package of rotary cutter blades, and an extra pair of sharp scissors. And always keep a healthy supply of pins and hand-sewing needles handy. Check your stash periodically and replenish your supplies before running out.

chapter 2

Getting Started

In *Sew Simple Squares,* you won't find any complicated patterns to trace and cut out. What you will find is a wide range of projects using simple sewing techniques, fabric layering, and easy folds to create beautiful home accents. The possibilities are endless and I'm sure you'll be more than satisfied with the results.

The projects in this book all begin with a simple fabric square. Fabric squares can be bought, recycled, or cut from larger pieces of fabric. Make your decision based on the materials available, as well as the desired look of your finished project.

readymade squares

Precut fabric squares, such as bandannas, wash-cloths, handkerchiefs, and napkins can be used to make many of the projects in this book. These are items most do-it-yourself home decorators have on hand, or they can be easily purchased from department and home decorating stores.

Bandannas are available in a wide array of colors and patterns, including paisley, floral, animal, and holiday prints. They can be purchased new or recycled from your wardrobe. Likewise, fabric handkerchiefs are attractively priced and plentiful, with something for every taste. Sometimes the handkerchiefs are reversible, making them ideal for projects like window treatments.

Save cutting time by using readymade fabric squares, such as bandannas, washcloths, handkerchiefs, and nap-kins to make the projects in this book.

A vintage napkin hung on point makes an attractive yet simple table topper. Scout flea markets and tag sales for antique linens to decorate your home.

Antique household linens are attractive choices for many decorating projects. Square linen napkins can be found in sizes ranging from 10 to 16 inches. They can have all-over patterns, corner motifs, or decorative borders.

Flea markets and yard sales are good sources for nicely preserved hankies and household linens. If you are planning a project using a number of flea-market finds, take a sample square of fabric along when shopping to match colors and sizes.

cutting squares

While working with readymade fabric squares is an inventive and fun way to jump-start your project, the selection is limited in regard to sizes, textures, and patterns available. Learning how to cut your own fabric squares will allow you to take advantage of a wide range of fabrics. In addition, you can cut squares from fabric leftover from other home sewing projects to customize your decorating scheme.

Using a square acrylic ruler with a rotary cutter and self-healing mat is by far the simplest way to cut a fabric square. When all three tools are used together, cutting time is minimal and the perfect square will be the end result.

If a rotary is not available, you can use a fabric marker and straightedge to measure your square. After marking, carefully cut out the square using sharp fabric scissors. When cutting squares with scissors, use long cuts to ensure even edges.

PREPARING FABRIC

Fabric preparation can be approached in several ways, depending on personal preference and fabric requirements. Unwashed fabric can be used, but should be ironed before cut. To remove sizing, allow for shrinkage, and test for color-fastness, most cottons and cotton blends should be pretreated as follows:

- Prewash fabric in warm water with a mild detergent and rinse several times in clear water. Do not use fabric that continues to bleed after several rinsings.

- Press fabric before cutting to ensure greater accuracy. Press on the wrong side of the fabric, following the fabric grain.

ROTARY CUTTING

Rotary cutters will cut up to six layers of fabric. Practice with various amounts of fabric to determine the number of layers you are comfortable cutting.

- Press fabrics before cutting. Lay fabric on a self-healing cutting mat, keeping the grain parallel to the marked grid.

- Lay a ruler on the fabric, to the left of the desired cutting line (unless you are right handed). Spread your hand out wide on the ruler and press down firmly.

- Place the rotary cutter against the ruler and push gently downward to cut through all layers. Hold the cutter upright, perpendicular to the cutting surface.

- Roll the cutter forward, away from the body, in a natural extension of the arm. Keep fingers, hands, and arms away from the cutting edge.

- If the fabric is longer than your ruler, exert pressure on the ruler and slide it across the fabric as you cut.

- For safety, always disengage the blade and return it to its housing after each cut.

- Keep spare replacement blades on hand. Replace a blade when it doesn't cut through all layers and when cutting produces ragged edges.

general directions

Folding and Pressing

Folded edges can be precisely measured along the entire foldline or simply at the initial fold, depending on your level of confidence and comfort. For utmost accuracy, use a sewing gauge to measure hems and folds. Mark the fold with pins or a chalk pencil, placing the marks every 2 to 3 inches around the hem. Once the line is established, press with an iron to secure the fold. (Be careful not to press over any pins.)

Pressing is important as it sets stitches and allows sewing projects to lie flat. Unlike ironing where you glide the iron across the fabric, to "press," you lift the iron up and put it back down in an overlapping pattern. For best results, select a steam iron with multiple fabric settings. Press each seam as it is sewn, using light to moderate pressure.

Layering Squares

One of the techniques often used in this book is layering. You can layer squares of different or equal sizes in various ways to achieve distinct design effects. When layering, the corners of the squares can be aligned, or you may choose to set the corners of each layer at a 90-degree angle, or "on point." A combination of layering techniques can also be used creatively. Bear in mind that the more complex the layering, the more planning and measuring required.

Layer two to four fabric squares at different angles to create depth and color separation. Vary the fabrics, sizes, and angles to create an infinite variety of looks.

Seams

A seam is where two pieces of fabric, usually right sides facing, are joined together with a straight stitch. The amount of fabric between the cut edge and seam is referred to as the "seam allowance." Seam allowances can vary from ¼ inch to ⅝ inch, depending on the fabric type and weight and the demands of the individual project. I used a variety of seam allowances for the projects in this book.

Stitch seams in the direction of the fabric grain to prevent stretching. To avoid tying a knot, backstitch at the beginning and end of a seam to secure the stitching. For narrow seams, secure the folded edge with two rows of stitching, or finish the seam with an overlock stitch (see "Stitch Glossary," page 32).

MITERING CORNERS

Finished corners can be mitered or joined at 45-degree angles by folding the tip of the corner down, then folding the two sides together so that they meet and are aligned. Press each fold to sharpen the corner.

1. To miter corners, first fold each adjacent fabric edge to the inside and press. Where the foldlines intersect, fold the tip of the fabric corner down and press.

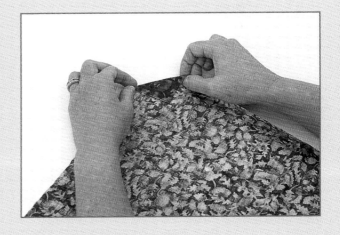

2. Next, fold over the long edges again, matching the inside edges with the folded tip and keeping the outside corner even. Press to secure the folds.

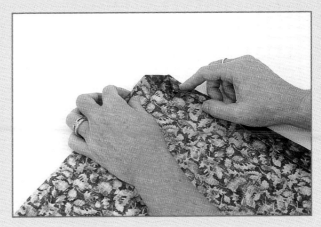

STITCH GLOSSARY

This quick reference guide will help introduce you to some of the basic machine- and hand-stitches used in this book. Note that for photography purposes, contrasting threads have been used in some illustrations. When sewing your projects, select thread colors that match or blend with your fabric. For machine stitching, always refer to your sewing machine manual for specific instructions.

Backstitch: Used at the beginning and end of stitching to secure threads and prevent seams from unraveling. To machine backstitch, straight-stitch forward, then in reverse, then forward again. To backstitch by hand, bring the needle through the fabric to the upper side. Take a small stitch back (about ⅛ inch), and then bring it back out again, about ⅛ inch forward.

Overlock stitch: Also known as "overedge" or "overcast" stitches, these stitches are used to prevent edges from raveling and curling. There are a variety of overlock stitch patterns that can be used, depending on your sewing machine. To overlock stitch by hand, insert the needle perpendicular to the edge of the fabric and stitch diagonally over the edge. Keep stitches a uniform depth and distance apart.

Satin stitch: This is a dense zigzag stitch that creates a shiny, satiny appearance because the stitches lie close together. Used for buttonholes and decorations, satin stitches can be done by hand as well as by machine. To satin stitch by machine, set the machine for a zigzag stitch with a small stitch length. To satin stitch by hand, bring the needle in and out of the fabric in very close, parallel stitches.

Slipstitch: A small hand-stitch used to invisibly secure or close off a folded edge of fabric or opening. Using a single strand of thread and a sewing needle, slide the needle through the folded fabric edge and pick up several fibers from the underneath fabric.

Straight stitch: The most basic and most important stitch in both hand- and machine-sewing. For hand sewing, a single thread is drawn in a straight line through the front of the fabric, then back through to the front again to bond two layers together. For machine sewing, a top thread is drawn through the fabric and looped with a bobbin (or bottom) thread.

Whipstitch: A hand stitch used to hold two finished edges together, such as a ribbon trim to fabric. Insert the needle at a right angle from the back edge to the front edge, picking up one or two threads at a time.

Zigzag stitch: A machine stitch that draws the thread back and forth in a "Z" pattern. Use a short, wide zigzag stitch to decoratively sew on trims or to encase raw edges of fabric.

A wide variety of embroidery stitches are available on disc, through internet sites, and on sewing machines. Use decorative stitches to enhance any project.

Decorative Stitches

Today's sewing machines offer an array of decorative embroidery stitches that, like satin stitching, can be substituted for many of the stitches shown in this book. Choose from blanket, cross, and honeycomb stitches, among others. There are also several straight-stitch and satin-stitch designs, such as a scallop or shell edging, that can be used for embellishment.

Hand embroidery is another decorative option. To hand embroider, use embroidery floss or a specialty thread, such as pearl cotton. Choose a needle that matches the thread and fabric being used. Refer to an embroidery stitch guide for basic guidelines.

Using Fusibles

A fusible bond is intended to be a permanent one. Before fusing, always refer to the manufacturer's guidelines for proper use. For best results, test-fuse before beginning your project. Set the iron for wool and steam, then adjust the settings as needed to find the best fusing temperature. Do not glide the iron back and forth, but lift and lower it into each position, applying a downward pressure for about ten to fifteen seconds. For the best bond, use a dampened or misted press cloth to soften the adhesive. Then, press the wrong and then the right side of your project to draw the adhesive into the fabric. Let the fabric cool completely before handling. To check the bond, try to pull the layers apart, then roll, fold, and examine the fabric.

APPLYING TRIMS

Trims can be used to add color and defini-
tion to a project. They can be applied with
fabric glue, fusible web, or hand- or
machine-stitching. Many trims, such as
banded tassels and ball fringe, are available with decorative headings. Pin these
trims face up on the fabric and machine-
or hand-stitch through the heading to
secure in place.

- To apply piping, pin the trim on the
  right side of the fabric with raw edges
  even. Overlap the ends by 1 inch. Cut
  open one end and remove 1 inch of
  cording. Fold under the cut edge and
  pin it overlapping the opposite end.
  Place the second fabric piece face
  down over the first. Using a zipper
  foot, sew through all layers as close to
  the cording as possible.

- To apply rickrack, pin one end in position and, holding the length loosely,
  topstitch along the center.

- To secure a flat trim, such as a ribbon
  or braid, pin the trim face up on the
  right side of the fabric. Stitch along
  both edges, working in the same direction. Flat trims used for embellishments
  can also be glued or hand-stitched
  in place.

- To apply a ruffle, pin the ruffle around
  the project top, with right sides facing
  and raw edges even. Pin the second
  fabric piece face down over the first
  and sew through all layers.

**Fabric squares in multiple colors or squares that
are not perfectly aligned can be unified and lined
up with colorful trims.**

APPLYING FRINGE

1. To apply fringe, place the fringe on the right side of the fabric square, with the straight edge of the trim even with the raw edge of the fabric. Fold under 1 inch on each end and pin so the ends meet but do not overlap. For corners, fold the excess trim on a diagonal and pin flat; hand-stitch the corner folds.

2. Place the second fabric square face down over the first, sandwiching the trim between the layers. Pin in place, then seam through all layers.

chapter 3

Pillows

Pillows are a great way to soften and add visual interest to any seating area. While lending comfort, they can also be used to bring together diverse fabric colors and patterns to harmonize a room's decor. Most pillow covers are essentially two squares seamed together and stuffed—couldn't be simpler! On the following pages you'll find pillows in an assortment of styles, from casual patchwork bolsters to elegant velvet throw pillows. Vary the designs with coordinating fabrics and trims to create your own unique looks.

simple square pillow

A simple square of fabric embellished with lavish trims can make a grand statement. This project is so easy to do even a first-time sewer can achieve fabulous results. Substitute fabrics and trims to create an endless variety of stylish pillows.

SKILL LEVEL Beginner

FINISHED SIZE
Two 15-inch-square pillows

WHAT YOU'LL NEED

Fabric

½ yard green chenille
½ yard yellow silk velvet

Supplies

62 inches of gold bullion fringe
60 inches of 1-inch gold gimp
60 inches of 1½-inch cream and green striped ribbon
62 inches of gold cording
Two 15-inch-square pillow forms
Green and gold thread
Sewing needle
Straight pins

Tools

Rotary cutter
Cutting mat
16½-inch-square clear acrylic ruler
Straightedge ruler or sewing gauge
Iron and ironing board
Scissors
Sewing machine

1. Using a rotary cutter and square ruler, cut two 16-inch squares from both the velvet and chenille fabrics.

2. For the chenille pillow, cut two 16-inch strips of ribbon and four 16-inch strips of gimp. Using the photograph as a guide, position the trims approximately 2½ inches from the top outside edges of one chenille square, leaving approximately ¼-inch to ½-inch spaces between the trims. Pin the trims in place, then sew along the outside edges using a matching thread.

3. Pin fringe along the edges of the chenille pillow front (see "Applying Trims," page 34). With right sides together, pin the chenille pillow front to the pillow back, sandwiching the fringe in between. Sew with a ½-inch seam, leaving a 6-inch opening. Turn the pillow cover right side out, insert a pillow form, then whipstitch the opening closed (see "Stitch Glossary," page 32).

4. For the velvet pillow, follow the same steps as above, except apply 16-inch strips of ribbon in a crisscross pattern on the right side of one velvet square. Trim the edges of the pillow front with cording, then seam and finish as described in Step 3.

split square pillow

This sweet and simple pillow design is made by piecing two fabric triangles. For a striking look, combine a striped and plaid fabric to contrast the diagonal lines. Complement the strong design with colorful textured trims.

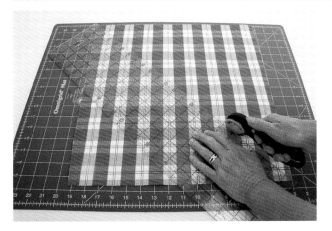

1. Using the rotary cutter and square ruler, cut one 15-inch square each of corduroy and plaid fabric and three 15-inch squares of floral stripe fabric. Cut the corduroy, plaid, and one floral fabric square diagonally in half.

2. Sew the long cut edges of two contrasting fabric triangles, right sides together with a ½-inch seam. Repeat the step to make two pieced squares. Press the seams open flat.

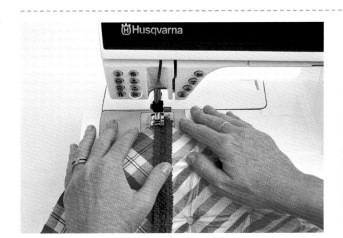

3. Cut each color of gimp to a 22-inch length. Sew a length over the front diagonal seam of each pillow.

4. For each pillow, layer the pillow front and floral pillow back, right sides facing, with fringe edging sandwiched in between the layers (see "Applying Trims," page 34). Sew with a ½-inch seam, leaving a 6-inch opening for turning. Turn right side out, insert the pillow form, and whip-stitch the opening closed (see "Stitch Glossary," page 32).

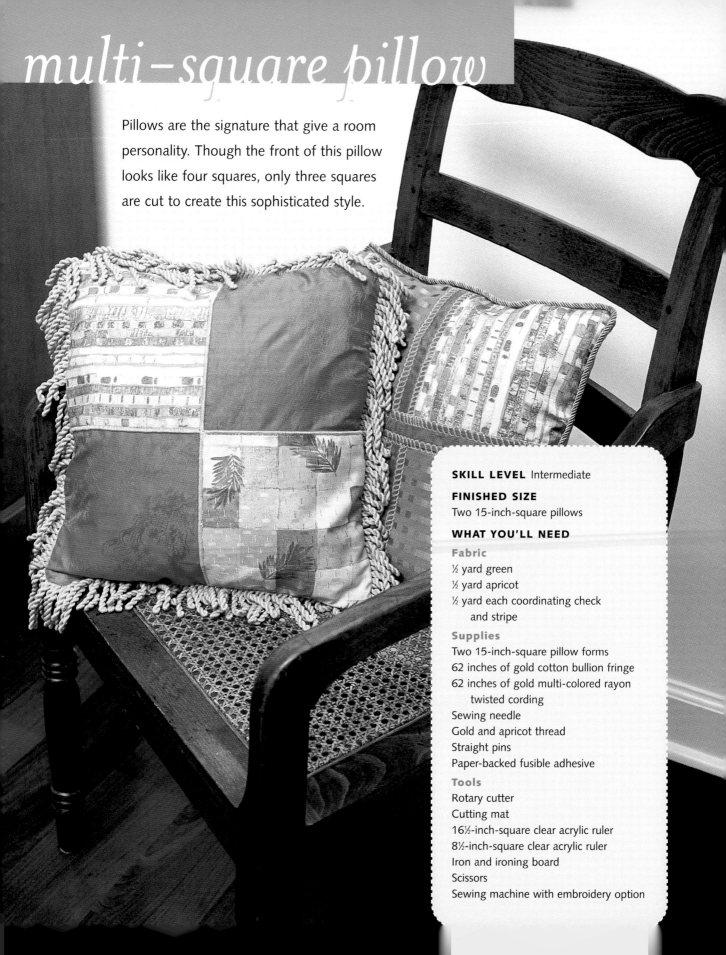

multi–square pillow

Pillows are the signature that give a room personality. Though the front of this pillow looks like four squares, only three squares are cut to create this sophisticated style.

SKILL LEVEL Intermediate

FINISHED SIZE
Two 15-inch-square pillows

WHAT YOU'LL NEED

Fabric
½ yard green
½ yard apricot
½ yard each coordinating check
    and stripe

Supplies
Two 15-inch-square pillow forms
62 inches of gold cotton bullion fringe
62 inches of gold multi-colored rayon
    twisted cording
Sewing needle
Gold and apricot thread
Straight pins
Paper-backed fusible adhesive

Tools
Rotary cutter
Cutting mat
16½-inch-square clear acrylic ruler
8½-inch-square clear acrylic ruler
Iron and ironing board
Scissors
Sewing machine with embroidery option

1. Cut two 16-inch squares each from the green and apricot fabrics. Cut two 8-inch squares each from the coordinating stripe and check fabrics. For the apricot pillow, iron fusible adhesive onto two coordinating 8-inch squares. Peel off the paper backing and iron the small squares onto one apricot square, as shown (see "Using Fusibles," page 33).

2. Satin stitch over the inside raw edges of the small squares (see "Stitch Glossary," page 32).

3. With right sides together, layer the pillow front, fringe, and pillow back (see "Applying Trims," page 34). Sew with a ½-inch seam, leaving a 6-inch opening for turning. Turn right side out, insert the pillow form, and slipstitch the opening closed.

4. For the green pillow, follow the same steps as above to apply the coordinating squares to the pillow front. Cut two 16- by 2-inch strips of apricot fabric. Fold the long edges under ½ inch and press. Position the strips over the inside raw edges of the small squares and sew in place with a decorative stitch.

raw edge bolster and matching pillow

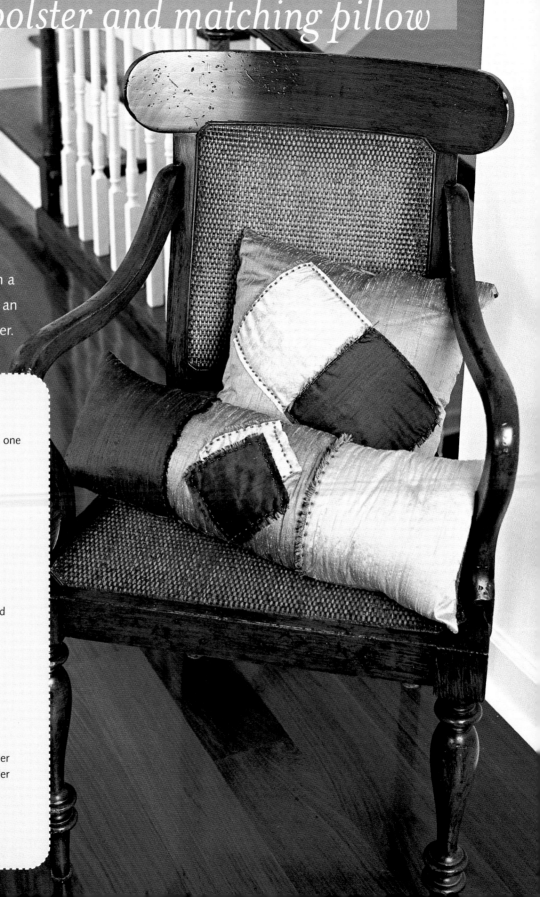

Nothing says comfort like a soft and silky bolster. Toss this luxurious bolster and matching pillow set on a sofa or chair to create an inviting and cozy corner.

SKILL LEVEL Intermediate

FINISHED SIZE
One 26- by 9-inch bolster and one 15-inch-square pillow

WHAT YOU'LL NEED

Fabric
½ yard gold silk
¼ yard beige silk
¼ yard brown silk

Supplies
Batting
15-inch-square pillow form
Beige and brown sewing thread
Black beading thread
Iridescent green seed beads
Beading needle
Sewing needle
Paper-backed fusible adhesive

Tools
Rotary cutter
Cutting mat
9½-inch-square clear acrylic ruler
4½-inch-square clear acrylic ruler
24-inch clear acrylic ruler
Iron and ironing board
Scissors
Sewing machine

1. For the bolster, cut one 9-inch square from each color of silk. Cut one 4¼-inch square each from the brown and beige silk. Cut one 27½- by 9½-inch rectangle from the gold silk.

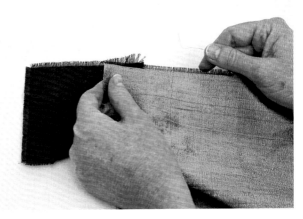

2. Fray the raw edges of each small 4¼-inch square by carefully removing the silk threads from each edge until you reach a depth of approximately ¼ inch. (If needed, use a straight pin to remove the threads.) Fray two opposite sides of each large square in the same manner.

3. Iron fusible adhesive onto each small square (see "Using Fusibles," page 33). Remove the paper backing, then position and iron the small squares overlapping and on point onto the large gold square.

4. With wrong sides together, sew the 9½-inch gold square to the 9½-inch brown square along the left edge with a ¼-inch seam. Open the fabric, then sew the beige 9½-inch square to the gold square in the same manner along the right edge.

5. Straight stitch ¼ inch from the frayed edges of the small squares. Thread 2 beads at a time onto the beading needle and sew beads around the perimeter of the small squares and along the seams. Space the beads approximately ¼ inch to ½ inch apart.

6. With right sides together, pin the pieced pillow front to the gold rectangle and sew with a ¼-inch seam, leaving a 6-inch opening for turning. Turn the cover right side out. Roll up a sheet of batting and insert it in the cover. Slipstitch the opening closed (see "Stitch Glossary," page 32).

7. For the pillow, cut two 16-inch squares from the gold silk, and two 6-inch squares from the beige and brown silk. Fuse the small squares to one gold square, positioning the squares so they are adjacent, as shown. Embellish the squares with beads, then stitch the pillow front to the back with a ½-inch seam, leaving a 6-inch opening. Turn right side out, insert the pillow form, and slipstitch the opening closed.

bandanna envelope pillow

This project transforms an everday bandanna and dishtowel into a comfy pillow. The envelope style is a popular trend that is achieved simply by layering and seaming cut squares. Dress the pillow up with trim and buttons for extra polish.

1. For the smaller pillow, cut one plaid towel and the muslin bandanna into 15-inch squares. Cut one corner of the paisley bandanna 11 inches from the point.

2. Fold the uncut edges of the bandanna 1 inch to the wrong side of the fabric and press. Straight stitch along the folded edges.

3. Glue trim along the folded edges of the bandanna, and then hand-sew one button on the point, as shown.

4. Pin the trimmed bandanna to the plaid square, right sides up with the cut edge of the bandanna evenly centered on one edge of the square. Pin the muslin square to the pillow front, right sides facing and edges even. Sew through all layers with a ½-inch seam, leaving a 6-inch opening. Trim off the excess fabric. Turn right side out, insert the 14-inch pillow form, and whipstitch the opening closed (see "Stitch Glossary," page 32).

5. For the larger pillow, cut two 17-inch squares from the remaining two plaid towels. Follow the steps above, replacing the napkin for the brown bandanna. Cut the washcloth in half on point from the corner and layer it on the napkin, as shown. Stitch along the edges to secure in place. Glue ½-inch brown and ¼-inch natural cording around the edge of the cloth. Finish as above, trimming the seam with ¼-inch brown cording (see "Applying Trims," page 34).

chapter 4

Bed Covers

Fabric squares become building blocks for creating fabulous bed covers. Despite their sophisticated appearance, the covers featured in this chapter are surprisingly simple to sew and can be made to blend with any interior, from a child's nursery to an adult's bedroom. The designs can be fitted for any size bed by enlarging or shortening the squares, or by eliminating or seaming on additional rows. Combine fabrics of various patterns and colors to create your own intriguing patterns.

baby blue crib cover

Big squares on a small crib can create an adorable bed cover. Use bright, contrasting colors and trim each square with rickrack to make a family heirloom that will be cherished for years to come. Add a third fabric and alter the size of the squares to make a full-size bed covering, as pictured on page 51.

SKILL LEVEL Beginner

FINISHED SIZE
One 46- by 34½-inch crib cover

WHAT YOU'LL NEED

Fabric
2 yards yellow and white print
1¼ yards blue and white check

Supplies
16 yards of white rickrack
Craft or crib size sheet of cotton
   quilt batting
Sewing needle
Yellow and blue rayon thread
White cotton thread
Straight pins

Tools
Rotary cutter
Cutting mat
6-inch-square clear acrylic ruler
12½-inch-square clear acrylic ruler
Iron and ironing board
Scissors
Sewing machine

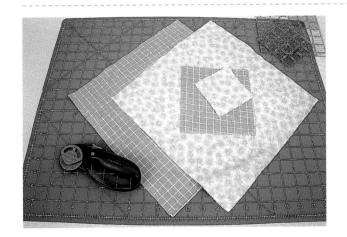

1. Using the rotary cutter and square rulers, cut the blue fabric into six 12½-inch and six 6-inch squares. Cut the yellow fabric into six 12½-inch and six 3½-inch squares.

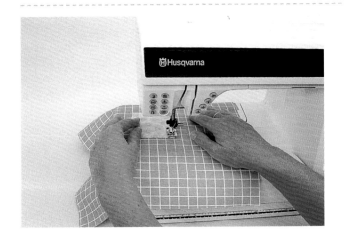

2. On the small 3½-inch yellow and 6-inch blue squares, fold the raw edges under ¼ inch to the wrong side and press. Center and pin the small yellow squares onto the large blue squares. Sew along the folded edges with an embroidery stitch.

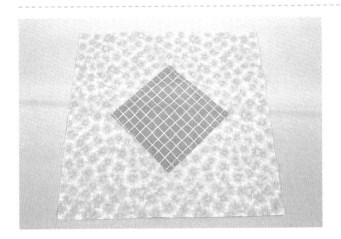

3. Center and pin the small blue squares on point onto the large yellow squares, as shown. Sew along the folded edges with an embroidery stitch.

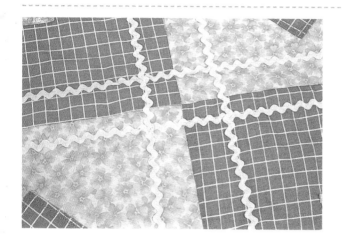

4. Alternating blue and yellow squares, sew 4 rows of 3 squares using a ½-inch seam. Sew the rows together with a ½-inch seam, alternating colors as shown. Sew rickrack approximately 1 inch from each side of each seam, going vertically and horizontally as shown (see "Applying Trims," page 34).

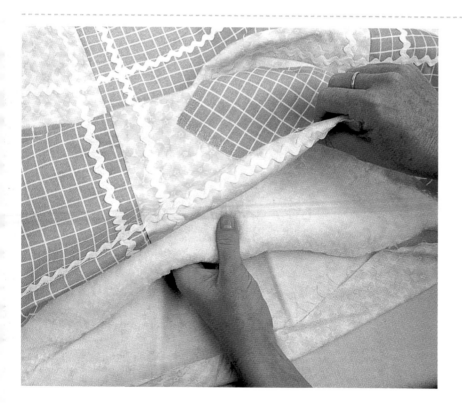

5. Cut the yellow fabric to the size of the pieced cover. Sew the front and back of the cover, right sides together and edges aligned, using a ½-inch seam and leaving a 20-inch opening. Turn the cover right side out. Cut the batting to size and insert it in the cover. Whipstitch the opening closed (see "Stitch Glossary," page 32).

floral spring bed cover

Pretty squares of polka dots, florals, and stripes sewn together create a warm and delicate look for any bed. For best results, choose fabrics with matching color schemes in prints that flatter and do not compete with each other. Consider picking up a fabric from your window covering for a harmonious effect.

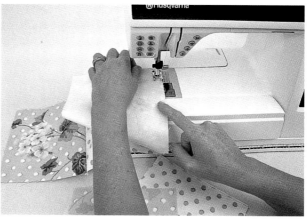

1. Using the rotary cutter and square ruler, cut the polka dot fabric into forty-nine 6½-inch squares. Cut the stripe fabric into forty-three 6½-inch squares. Cut the floral fabric into forty 6½-inch squares.

2. Using a ¼-inch seam allowance, make 5 rows by sewing 9 squares together in order: polka dot to floral. Make 5 rows by sewing 9 squares together in order: stripe to polka dot.

3. When all of the rows are complete, sew a floral square on each end of the stripe and polka dot rows, and a stripe square on each end of the floral and polka dot rows.

4. Make 2 rows by sewing 9 squares together in order: floral and stripe. Sew a polka dot square at each end of each floral and stripe row. Press all rows and sew them together so end rows alternate from dot to stripe to floral, as shown.

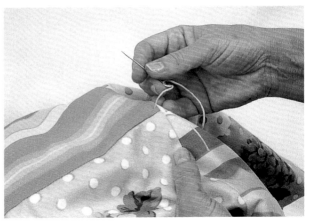

5. Cut the sheet and quilt batting to the size of the bed cover. Sew the top and bottom covers with right sides together and edges even, leaving a 20-inch opening along one edge. Turn right side out, insert the batting, and whipstitch the opening closed (see "Stitch Glossary," page 32). Press the seams flat.

6. With the embroidery needle and six strands of embroidery floss, working at 6- or 12-inch intervals, sew through all layers of the bed cover and tie off (see "Tying-Off," below).

TYING-OFF

Tying-off is a fast method of securing the layers of a bed cover together. In addition, it enhances the cover with the sculptured look of quilting. Use a large-eye needle and embroidery floss or ribbon to tie-off. Insert the needle from the front side of the design and stitch through all layers. Then, turn the needle and stitch back through all layers to return to the front. Cut the floss, leaving approximately 1-inch ends, then tie the ends in a tight square knot

chenille bedspread

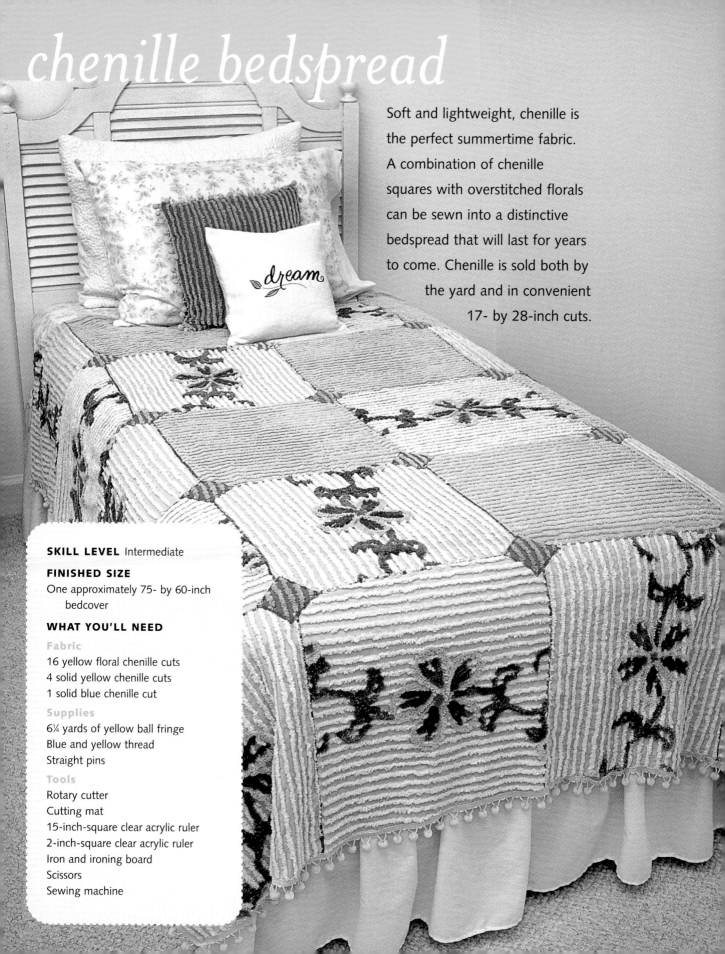

Soft and lightweight, chenille is the perfect summertime fabric. A combination of chenille squares with overstitched florals can be sewn into a distinctive bedspread that will last for years to come. Chenille is sold both by the yard and in convenient 17- by 28-inch cuts.

SKILL LEVEL Intermediate

FINISHED SIZE
One approximately 75- by 60-inch bedcover

WHAT YOU'LL NEED

Fabric
16 yellow floral chenille cuts
4 solid yellow chenille cuts
1 solid blue chenille cut

Supplies
6¼ yards of yellow ball fringe
Blue and yellow thread
Straight pins

Tools
Rotary cutter
Cutting mat
15-inch-square clear acrylic ruler
2-inch-square clear acrylic ruler
Iron and ironing board
Scissors
Sewing machine

Note: When sewing chenille, it is better to push the fabric toward the presser foot, rather than letting it feed.

1. Using the rotary cutter and square rulers, cut sixteen 15-inch floral squares, four 15-inch yellow squares, and sixteen 2-inch blue squares.

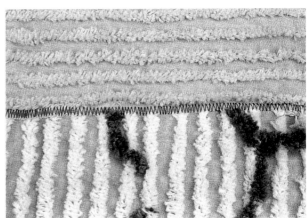

2. With blue thread and a zigzag stitch, sew the squares together by slightly overlapping the raw edges approximately ¼ inch (see "Stitch Glossary," page 32). Using the photograph as a pattern guide, make 5 rows of 4 squares, then join the rows, as shown.

3. Position and pin the small blue squares on point over each intersection of squares. Sew the small blue squares in place using a zigzag stitch.

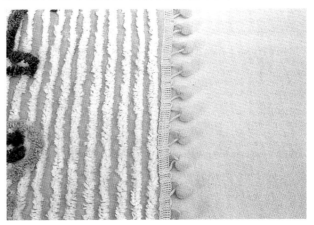

4. Fold all raw edges under ¼ inch and press. Sew along the edges with an overcast stitch. Using yellow thread, sew ball fringe along one short and two long edges of the bedspread (see "Applying Trims," page 34).

chapter 5

Decorative Touches

Decorative fabric accents enhance any interior design with pattern, color, and texture. As only small squares are needed, feel free to indulge in luxurious textiles and trims. Consider using remnants leftover from other home decorating projects, or mix and match an assortment of patterns for a lively presentation. The following are just a few fun ideas to dress up your home. Let them inspire you to create your own imaginative designs.

layered picture frame

Layer squares of fabric over a picture frame to create a one-of-a-kind photo holder. Follow the directions to decorate a new frame or refurbish an old one, or build the holder from scratch using a mat board base. If you fear damaging a treasured photo, use acid-free photo mount corners instead of fusible adhesive.

SKILL LEVEL Beginner

FINISHED SIZE
One 11- by 12½-inch frame

WHAT YOU'LL NEED

Fabric
½ yard green and red plaid
6-inch remnant of red check

Supplies
Approximately 2½- by 3½-inch
   photograph
1½ yards of 1-inch red grosgrain
   ribbon
11- by 12½-inch flat-faced wooden
   craft picture frame
Four 1-inch brown buttons
5-inch-square mat board
Cotton batting
Paper-backed fusible adhesive
Sheet of paper
Sewing needle
Red thread
Fabric glue

Tools
Heavy-duty staple gun and staples
Rotary cutter
Cutting mat
12½-inch-square clear acrylic ruler
16½-inch-square clear acrylic ruler
Iron and ironing board
Scissors
Sewing machine

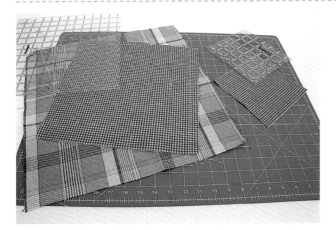

1. With the rotary cutter and square rulers, cut one 16-inch green plaid square, and one 12½-inch and one 6-inch red check square. Cut cotton batting to fit the frame.

2. Center the batting and the green plaid square onto the front side of the frame.

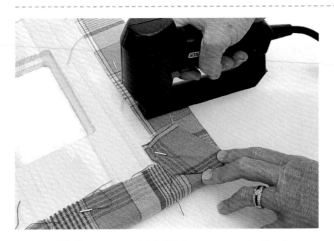

3. Fold the green plaid fabric over to the back side of the frame and staple along the edges, working from opposite ends and smoothing the fabric as you go. Fold the corners smooth and flat and staple in place.

4. Iron adhesive onto the wrong side of the 6-inch red check square (see "Using Fusibles," page 33). Remove the paper backing, center the fabric onto the mat board, and fuse in place. Wrap the fabric edges to the back of the mat board and iron to secure.

5. With the iron on a low setting, iron adhesive onto the back side of the photograph, applying even pressure and working from the center outwards. (Practice applying fusible adhesive to a discard print before working on the actual photograph.)

6. Center the photograph on the front side of the covered mat board. Lay a sheet of paper over the surface of the photo for protection. With the iron on a low setting and applying even pressure, fuse the photo to the mat board, working from the center outwards.

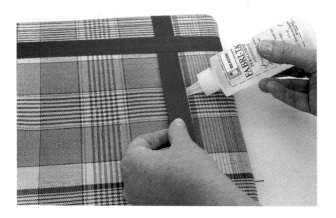

7. Cut two 16-inch and two 17-inch strips of ribbon. Position and glue the ribbons running first horizontally, then vertically to the front of the frame, approximately 2 inches from each edge. Wrap the ribbon ends to the back of the frame and glue in place.

8. Weave thread through the holes of each button. Knot the ends on the back and secure with a drop of glue. Glue a button at each intersection of the ribbons.

9. Fold under the edges of the 12½-inch red check square ½ inch to the wrong side and press. Straight stitch along the folded edges. Glue the square to the back of the frame, covering the raw edges of the green plaid fabric, as shown.

10. Center the mounted photograph onto the front side of the covered frame and glue in place. Allow the glue to dry before displaying the frame vertically.

tissue box cover

A simple 16-inch square of fabric can be transformed into a pretty tissue box cover in just a matter of minutes. While cleverly disguising an unappealing cardboard box, the fabric cover lends a graceful note to a home decorating scheme.

SKILL LEVEL Beginner

FINISHED SIZE
One 15- by 11-inch cover

WHAT YOU'LL NEED

Fabric
½ yard floral

Supplies
Standard 9¼-inch long, 3-inch high, and 4¾-inch wide rectangular tissue box
Two 1½-inch buttons
Sewing needle
Tan thread
Straight pins

Tools
Rotary cutter
Cutting mat
16-inch-square clear acrylic ruler
24-inch clear acrylic ruler
Iron and ironing board
Scissors
Sewing machine

1. Using the rotary cutter and square ruler, cut one 16-inch fabric square. Trim 4 inches off of one fabric edge to make a 16- by 12-inch piece of floral fabric.

2. Fold the raw edges under ½ inch to the wrong side and press. Sew two rows of straight stitches approximately ¼ inch and ⅜ inch from the folded edges. Press the stitching flat.

3. Center the fabric on the tissue box. With the scissors, cut an "x" in the fabric cover at the tissue box opening, as shown.

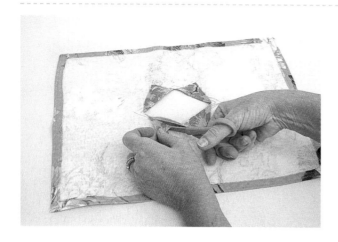

4. Remove the fabric from the box. Fold all four corners of the cut-out opening back to the wrong side and press. Sew around the opening with two rows of straight stitching, ¼ inch and ⅜ inch from the folded edges. Trim the excess fabric.

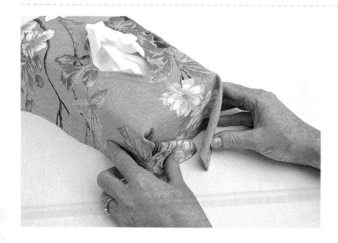

5. Position the fabric centered on the box. Fold, tuck, and pin the fabric at each box end, as shown.

6. Sew a button onto the center of each folded end to secure the cover in place.

embellished lampshade

Simple squares of fabric update a lampshade and transform it into a stunning decorative showpiece. For a customized look, match the fabric squares to the color scheme of your room, or cut the squares from scraps left over from slipcovers and curtains. Edge the shade with a braided trim for a more formal finish.

SKILL LEVEL Beginner

FINISHED SIZE
Four 4-inch-square embellishments

WHAT YOU'LL NEED

Fabric
⅛ yard red check
⅛ yard red and tan floral

Supplies
Medium-sized flat-sided lampshade
Fabric glue
Taupe thread
Paper-backed fusible adhesive

Tools
Rotary cutter
Cutting mat
4-inch-square clear acrylic ruler
2½-inch-square clear acrylic ruler
Iron and ironing board
Scissors
Sewing machine

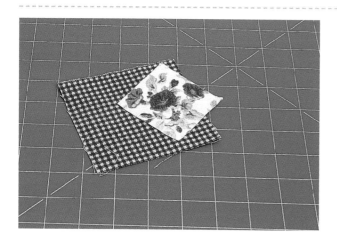

1. With the rotary cutter and square rulers, cut four 4-inch red check squares and four 2½-inch floral squares.

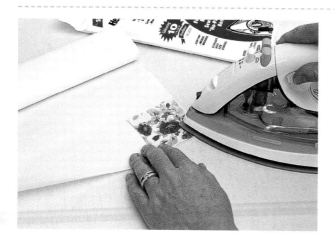

2. Iron adhesive to the wrong side of the small floral squares (see "Using Fusibles," page 33). Remove the paper backing and center each small square onto a large check square and fuse in place.

3. Sew decorative or zigzag stitches along the edges of the small floral squares (see "Stitch Glossary," page 32).

4. Fold the raw edges of each large square under approximately ⅛ inch to the wrong side and press. Overcast stitch along the folded edges (see "Stitch Glossary," page 32). Press the stitching flat.

5. Glue a square on point to each side of the lampshade, as shown.

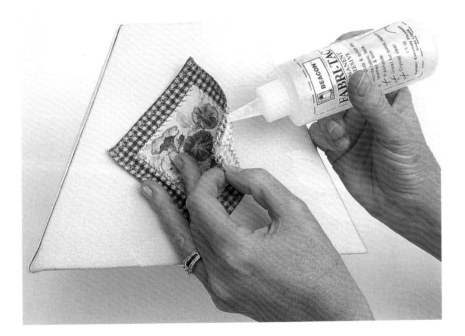

chapter 6

Chair Covers

Fabric squares give plain and purposeful chair backs a whole new dimension of design. These covers lend a soft layer of support while transforming everyday chairs into spectacular seating. Best of all, since only a minimum of sewing and piecing is required, you can quickly and easily whip up a whole set of covers to coordinate dining and living areas. Add distinctive trimmings, such as piping, ribbon, and braids, to express your personal style.

folded chair covers

SKILL LEVEL Beginner

FINISHED SIZE
Four 14½-inch-square covers

WHAT YOU'LL NEED

Fabric
½ yard blue and white plaid
½ yard blue and yellow floral

Supplies
Sewing needle
Yellow thread

Tools
Rotary cutter
Cutting mat
15-inch clear acrylic ruler
Iron and ironing board
Scissors
Sewing machine

Sew two squares of coordinated fabric together to create a versatile chair ensemble. Ideal for dressing up ladder-back chairs, this simple project will enhance any table setting. For a custom look, pair chair covers with tablecloths and linens sewn from matching fabric.

Note: Measure the chair back for a proper fit. Adjust the dimensions of the squares accordingly.

1. With the rotary cutter and ruler, cut four 15-inch squares from each fabric.

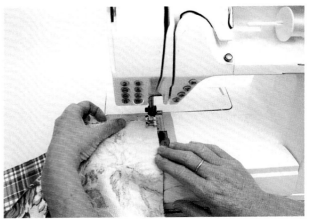

2. With right sides together, sew a plaid square to a floral square with a ¼-inch seam, leaving a 5-inch opening for turning. Turn the fabric right side out and press. Slipstitch the opening closed (see "Stitch Glossary," page 32). Repeat to make four seamed squares.

3. Straight stitch approximately ¼ inch inside each seamed edge. Press the stitching flat.

4. Fold over two opposite corners of each cover, as shown, then position each cover on point over a chair back slat.

chenille chair covers

Chenille lends texture and softness to this chair cover, while the floral and check embellishments add color and depth. This project is fast and easy and will enhance any seat, indoors or out.

SKILL LEVEL Beginner

FINISHED SIZE
One 17-inch-square cover

WHAT YOU'LL NEED

Fabric
Two 17- by 28-inch yellow
   chenille cuts
¼ yard red check
6-inch remnant floral

Supplies
Red rayon and yellow cotton
   thread
Straight pins

Tools
Rotary cutter
Cutting mat
6½-inch clear acrylic ruler
24-inch clear acrylic ruler
Iron and ironing board
Scissors
Sewing machine

Note: Measure the chair back for a proper fit. Adjust the dimensions of the squares accordingly.

1. With the rotary cutter and ruler, cut two 17-inch squares of chenille, one 6½-inch square of check fabric, and one 5¾-inch square of floral fabric. Cut five 17- by 3-inch strips of check fabric.

2. With right sides facing up, center and sew the floral square onto the check square using a satin stitch (see "Stitch Glossary," page 32). Center the stitched square onto a chenille square and sew in place using a satin stitch.

3. For trim, fold under the long edges of the fabric strips ¼ inch to the wrong side and press. Fold the strips in half lengthwise and press. Pin and sew a strip onto the bottom edge of each chenille square using a zigzag stitch.

4. Layer the chenille squares, wrong sides together and matching the bottom edges. Pin strips of trim encasing the top and two side edges of the two chenille squares. Sew the trim in place using a zigzag stitch, as shown.

saddle-style chair covers

I call this a saddle-style chair cover simply because the square rests on top of the cover, like a saddle on a horseback. Use this cover to give a plain, straight-back chair a timeless, masculine appeal.

Note: Measure the chair back for a proper fit. Adjust the dimensions of the squares accordingly.

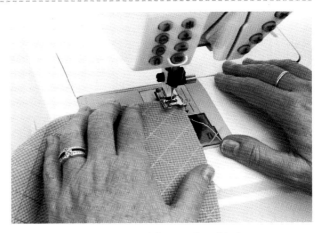

1. Cut one 14-inch square of paisley, centering the pattern on point. Cut one 22-inch square of gold fabric and two 22-inch squares of batting. Iron fusible adhesive to the wrong side of the paisley square (see "Using Fusibles," page 33). Remove the paper backing and center the square on point on the gold square; fuse in place.

2. Trim the corners of the paisley fabric even with the edges of the gold square. Fold the square in half with the right sides together and pin. Sew the short edges with a ½-inch seam. Turn the cover right side out.

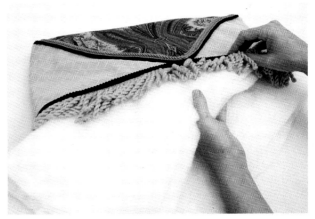

3. Sew bullion fringe along the open edges using a zigzag stitch (see "Applying Trims," page 34). Using the photograph as a guide, glue gimp and cording over the fringe heading and around the edges of the paisley square.

4. Layer and fold the batting squares in half. Insert the batting into the chair cover for padding. Slip the cover over the chair back, as shown on opposite page.

sofa back covers

Transform the look of any sofa with fashionable fabric covers. These striped covers, adorned with tassels and trim, add design interest and character to a basic white couch.

SKILL LEVEL Beginner

FINISHED SIZE
Three 20-inch-square covers

WHAT YOU'LL NEED

Fabric
1½ yards navy and white ticking

Supplies
3 navy tassels
6¾ yards of navy gimp
Blue thread
Sewing needle
Straight pins

Tools
Rotary cutter
Cutting mat
20-inch clear acrylic ruler
Iron and ironing board
Scissors
Sewing machine with embroidery
    option

Note: Measure the sofa back for a proper fit. Adjust the dimensions of the squares accordingly.

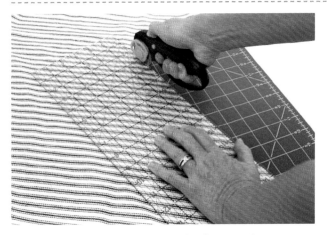

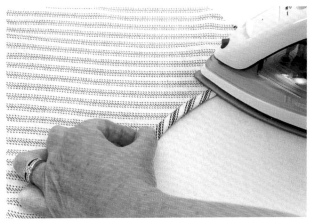

1. With the rotary cutter and ruler, cut three 20-inch squares of fabric, positioning the stripes so that they are running vertical on point.

2. Fold under the raw edges of each square to the wrong side ¼ inch, then ¼ inch again. Press the folds flat.

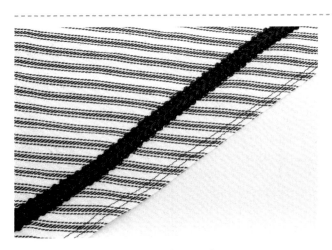

3. Sew two rows of straight stitching approximately ⅛ inch and ¼ inch from each folded edge. Press the stitching flat. Sew gimp approximately 1 to 1½ inches from each folded edge, as shown.

4. Coil the end of a tassel string into a spiral and sew the tassel on one corner point of one square. Repeat to sew a tassel to one corner of each remaining square. Position the squares on the sofa back, as shown on the opposite page.

chapter 7

Table Settings

Squares flatter round, square, and rectangular tables alike. They can be overlapped for a layered look, or pivoted for a dynamic effect. Position squares in the center of a table to create a lovely stage for a centerpiece, or join several squares across the length of a table to make a one-of-a-kind runner. All it takes is a simple change of fabric to switch the style and tone of your setting from traditional to modern. Consider making mats and runners in a variety of fabrics for seasonal makeovers and holiday get-togethers.

creative table runner

A little imagination will set any table to a "t." This runner, made from separate squares of blue and white check fabric, makes this table look even longer than it really is. A decorative embroidery stitch is used to unify the squares and give them an attractive finish.

SKILL LEVEL Beginner

FINISHED SIZE
Four 11½-inch squares

WHAT YOU'LL NEED

Fabric
1 yard blue and white check

Supplies
White rayon thread

Tools
Rotary cutter
Cutting mat
24-inch clear acrylic ruler
12½-inch-square clear acrylic ruler
Iron and ironing board
Scissors
Sewing machine with embroidery stitch option

1. With the rotary cutter and rulers, cut four 12½-inch squares and one 22-inch square of fabric.

2. Fold all of the raw edges under ½ inch to the wrong side and press. Miter all of the folded fabric corners (see "Mitering," page 31).

3. Sew an embroidery stitch approximately ½ inch from the folded edge, making sure to catch the raw edge in the stitching. Press the stitching flat.

4. Lay the squares on the tabletop on point, placing the largest square in the center. Adjust the squares so that the corner of each square overlaps the next, as shown.

summertime table setting

Summertime is a great time for bright and happy colors. Here, I've layered two vivid pink fabric squares over an aqua tablecloth to set the mood for a festive meal. Complement the mats with trims or ribbons, then top it all off with matching dinnerware.

SKILL LEVEL Beginner

FINISHED SIZES
Two 16½-inch-square and two 15-inch-square mats

WHAT YOU'LL NEED

Fabric
1 yard light pink print
1 yard dark pink print
Two 21-inch-square pink bandannas (for napkins)

Supplies
1 spool of ⅛-inch aqua satin ribbon
Pink and aqua thread

Tools
Rotary cutter
Cutting mat
24-inch clear acrylic ruler
16½-inch-square clear acrylic ruler
Iron and ironing board
Scissors
Sewing machine with ribbon feeder foot

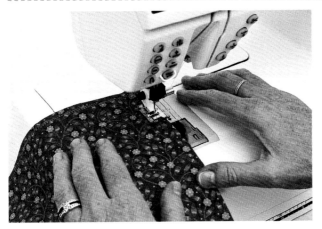

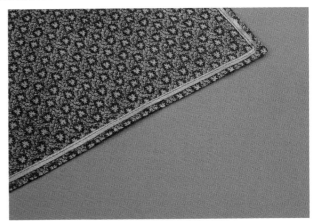

1. Cut the light pink fabric into two 17-inch squares and the dark pink fabric into two 16-inch squares. Fold all of the raw edges under ¼ inch to the wrong side and press. Fold the edges under ¼ inch again and press. With the aqua thread, sew the dark pink square with a zigzag stitch ⅛ inch from each folded edge (see "Stitch Glossary," page 32).

2. Using a ribbon feeder foot and matching thread, straight stitch ribbon on the light pink square approximately ⅛ inch from each folded edge.

3. Lay the light pink squares on the table with one point hanging over the table edge and the opposite point facing the center of the table. Lay the dark pink squares on top of the light pink squares, as shown.

4. For napkins, fold under one edge of each bandanna 1 inch and press. Fold the opposite edge in half, so that the edge tucks under the first fold. Press the folds flat. Fold and press each napkin with 1-inch accordion folds, as shown. Slip each napkin into a napkin ring to secure the folds.

golfer's delight table mats

This golf-themed table arrangement is terrific fun for sports-minded guys and gals. The rich brown and gold palette looks warm and welcoming and nicely complements the smooth wood tabletop. If golf is not your thing, look for fabrics with similar large-scale motifs to sew into place mats.

SKILL LEVEL Beginner

FINISHED SIZE
Four 16½-inch-square mats

WHAT YOU'LL NEED

Fabric
1 yard brown and gold check
1 yard golf-themed print

Supplies
Paper-backed fusible adhesive
Green and gold rayon thread
Straight pins

Tools
Rotary cutter
Cutting mat
16½-inch-square clear acrylic ruler
Iron and ironing board
Scissors
Sewing machine with embroidery option

Note: Yardage will be determined by the size and distance between the motifs. The golf motif used in this project measures approximately 12 inches square.

1. With the rotary cutter and ruler, cut the golf-print fabric into four 12½-inch squares, centering the design on each square. Cut the check fabric into four 16½-inch squares.

2. Iron fusible adhesive onto the wrong side of the golf-print square (see "Using Fusibles," page 33). Peel off the paper backing, then center and iron the golf-print square onto the check square, right sides facing up.

3. With the green thread, sew a decorative embroidery stitch around the raw edges of the golf square (see "Decorative Stitches," page 33). Press the stitching flat.

4. Fold the edges of the check fabric under ¼ inch to the wrong side and press. With the gold thread, sew a decorative stitch along the folded edges of the check square.

simple square tablecloth

A delightful combination of pink floral and plaid fabrics capture the beauty of a blooming summer garden. Ideal for a picnic or a casual Sunday brunch, this lovely topper has three layers of squares that support and showcase the pretty pink centerpiece.

SKILL LEVEL Beginner

FINISHED SIZE
One 43-inch-square tablecloth

WHAT YOU'LL NEED

Fabric
1½ yards floral
½ yard pink plaid

Supplies
Paper-backed fusible adhesive
Green rayon and white cotton thread

Tools
Rotary cutter
Cutting mat
12-inch-square clear acrylic ruler
24-inch clear acrylic ruler
Iron and ironing board
Scissors
Sewing machine with embroidery option

1. With the rotary cutter and ruler, cut one 18-inch plaid square and one 45-inch and one 12-inch floral square.

2. Iron adhesive onto the wrong side of the 18-inch and 12-inch squares (see "Using Fusibles," page 33). Peel off the paper backing, center the 12-inch square on the 18-inch square, right sides facing up, and fuse in place. Remove the paper backing and center the 18-inch square on the 45-inch square, right sides up, and fuse in place.

3. Using the green thread, sew a decorative embroidery stitch around the perimeters of the two smaller squares (see "Decorative Stitches," page 33).

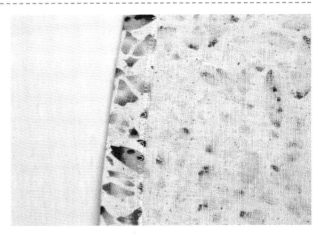

4. Fold the edges of the 45-inch square under approximately 1 inch and press. Sew along the raw edges with an overcast stitch (see "Stitch Glossary," page 32).

garden fresh place mats

SKILL LEVEL Beginner

FINISHED SIZE
Four 15½-inch-square mats

WHAT YOU'LL NEED

Fabric
½ yard green polka dot
½ yard floral

Supplies
Paper-backed fusible adhesive
Lavender and green rayon
    thread

Tools
Rotary cutter
Cutting mat
16½-inch-square clear
    acrylic ruler
Iron and ironing board
Scissors
Sewing machine with
    embroidery option

Even the most casual meal will feel like a celebration with these charming fabric place mats. The mats are simply made by layering squares of coordinating polka dot and floral fabrics, then embellishing with decorative embroidery stitches. Crown the settings with pretty ribbon bows for a feminine flourish.

1. With the rotary cutter and ruler, cut four 16½-inch floral squares and four 11-inch polka-dot squares.

2. Iron fusible adhesive onto the wrong side of each polka-dot square (see "Using Fusibles," page 33). Peel off the paper backing, then center and iron a polka-dot square on point onto each floral square, right sides facing up, as shown.

3. With lavender thread, sew a decorative embroidery stitch around the perimeter of the small squares (see "Decorative Stitches," page 33).

4. With green thread, sew a decorative embroidery stitch ¼ inch from the raw edges of each floral square. Trim the excess fabric outside of the stitching and press.

reversible place mats

Nothing complements a fine wood table like gold and black place mats. These sophisticated mats are surprisingly simple to make from two squares of contrasting fabric. Switch from the solid to the two-toned side for a quick style change.

SKILL LEVEL Beginner

FINISHED SIZE
Six 14-inch-square mats

WHAT YOU'LL NEED

Fabric
2 yards black damask
1½ yards gold print

Supplies
Black thread
Paper-backed fusible adhesive

Tools
Rotary cutter
Cutting mat
20-inch clear acrylic ruler
14½-inch-square clear acrylic ruler
Iron and ironing board
Scissors
Sewing machine

Note: Because the fabrics used for this project are heavyweight, I chose to overlap the corners; however, if you choose to use lightweight fabrics, you may miter the corners (see "Mitering," page 31). Contrasting thread is used for photography purposes only.

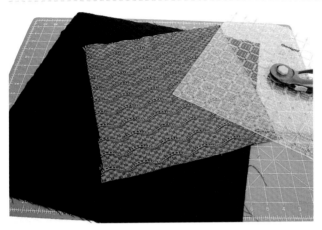

1. With the rotary cutter and ruler, cut six 18-inch black squares and six 14½-inch gold squares.

2. Iron fusible adhesive onto the wrong side of each gold square and remove the paper backing (see "Using Fusibles," page 33). Center each gold square on a black square, wrong sides together, and iron to adhere.

3. Working from opposite ends, fold the edges of each black square under ½ inch to the wrong side and press. Fold the edges under again approximately 1½ inches, so that the edges slightly overlap the gold square. Press the folds flat.

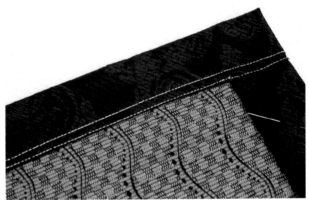

4. Sew along the inside edges of the black fabric with two rows of straight stitching, ¼ inch and ⅛ inch from each folded edge. Press the stitching flat.

chapter 8

Window Treatments

Nothing adds design interest to a window treatment like a valance. They can be blended with curtains for a discreet decoration, or made to contrast for an extra layer of color and pattern. This chapter shows you how to make valances from simple to sumptuous, working with both readymade as well as cut squares of fabric. You'll see how fabric squares can be joined to form a straight valance, or draped diagonally to make a triangular one. And if you don't want to hem or stitch, you can just knot a row of fabric squares to a curtain rod for a fun and breezy no-sew style.

simple overlay valance

SKILL LEVEL Beginner

FINISHED SIZE
Four 25-inch squares

WHAT YOU'LL NEED

Fabric
2½ yards red and tan
   check
2 yards coordinating blue
   floral

Supplies
Blue rayon and red cotton
   thread
Straight pins

Tools
Rotary cutter
Cutting mat
26-inch clear acrylic ruler
16½-inch-square clear
   acrylic ruler
Iron and ironing board
Scissors
Sewing machine with
   embroidery option

Layer and sew two sizes of fabric squares with different prints and colors to create a stylish, yet simple window valance. The valance can be made casual or dressy depending on the fabrics chosen. Quick-stitch an assortment of valances to update a room or for seasonal makeovers.

Note: This valance was designed for a 108-inch-wide window. Adjust the number or size of the squares as desired to fit your window opening.

1. With the rotary cutter and ruler, cut four 26-inch check squares and four 16½-inch floral squares. Press the fabric flat.

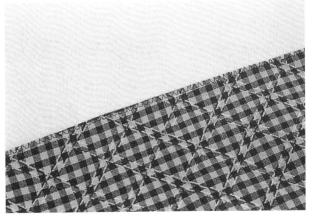

2. Fold the raw edges of each check square under ¼ inch to the wrong side and sew with an overcast stitch (see "Stitch Glossary," page 32). Press the stitching flat.

3. Center a floral square onto each check square, right sides facing up, and pin in place. With the blue embroidery thread, satin stitch along the outside edges of each floral square. Press the stitching flat.

4. Drape the finished squares on point over the curtain rod, overlapping the ends as shown.

button–fold valance

Solid and check fabric squares folded and buttoned create a clean and tailored-looking valance. Match fabrics to pillowcases and slipcovers to tie together a bedroom décor.

SKILL LEVEL Beginner

FINISHED SIZE
Three 15-inch squares

WHAT YOU'LL NEED

Fabric
½ yard yellow
½ yard yellow gingham

Supplies
Six ½-inch white buttons
Sewing needle
Yellow thread

Tools
Rotary cutter
Cutting mat
15½-inch-square clear
    acrylic ruler
Iron and ironing board
Scissors
Sewing machine

This valance was designed for a 36-inch-wide window. Adjust the number or size of the squares as desired to fit your window opening.

1. With the rotary cutter and ruler, cut three 15½-inch squares from both the solid yellow and yellow gingham fabrics.

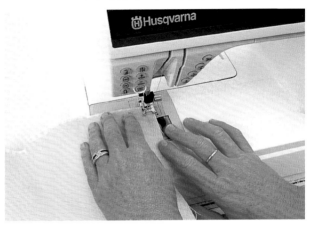

2. With the wrong sides together, sew a solid square to each check square, leaving a 4-inch opening for turning. Turn the squares right side out and press. Slipstitch the openings closed (see "Stitch Glosssary," page 32). Press the seams flat.

3. To make a casing, fold over the top edge of each square an equal distance to fit your curtain rod with room for ease. Press the folds flat. Slipstitch the folds to the back fabric and press.

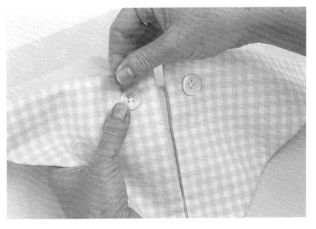

4. Fold up the bottom corners of each square to the center to create a point, as shown. Press the folds flat. Sew buttons approximately 1 inch from the inside corners, stitching through all layers of fabric to secure the folds.

napkin valance

SKILL LEVEL Beginner

FINISHED SIZE
Four 18-inch-square
napkins

WHAT YOU'LL NEED

Fabric
4 white linen napkins

Tools
Iron and ironing board

Antique linen napkins hung decoratively on a curtain rod create a delicate, Victorian-style valance. This is an incredibly easy, no-sew project that can be accomplished in just a few short minutes. If you don't have pretty linens on hand, they can be readily found in flea markets and thrift stores.

Note: This valance was designed for a 36-inch-wide window. Adjust the number or size of the napkins as desired to fit your window opening.

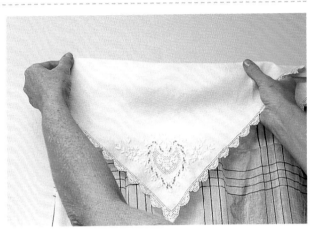

1. Lay each napkin out flat on the ironing board and press. Set two napkins aside. Lay the first remaining napkin on the board on point. Fold under and press one corner approximately 5 inches, as shown. Lay the second napkin out in the same manner. Fold the opposite corner under 5 inches and press.

2. Hang the folded napkins on opposite ends of the curtain rod, with the folded edges on each end.

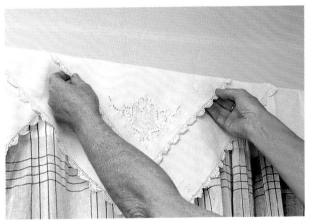

3. Position and hang the third napkin on point at the center of the curtain rod, overlapping the inside corners of both end napkins.

4. Hang the fourth napkin on point over the center napkin, so that the corner points are aligned and set approximately 4 inches apart, as shown.

toile valance

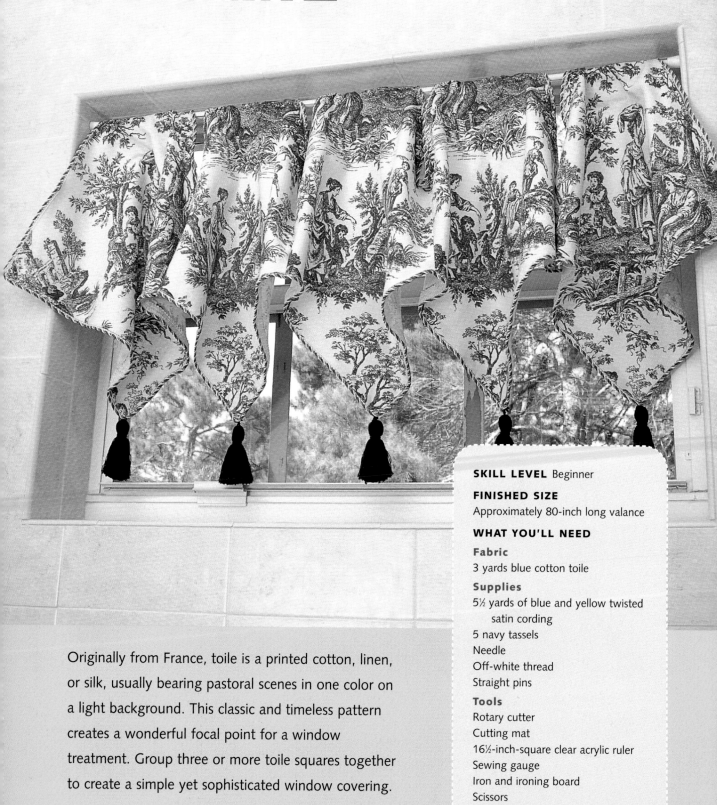

Originally from France, toile is a printed cotton, linen, or silk, usually bearing pastoral scenes in one color on a light background. This classic and timeless pattern creates a wonderful focal point for a window treatment. Group three or more toile squares together to create a simple yet sophisticated window covering.

SKILL LEVEL Beginner

FINISHED SIZE
Approximately 80-inch long valance

WHAT YOU'LL NEED

Fabric
3 yards blue cotton toile

Supplies
5½ yards of blue and yellow twisted satin cording
5 navy tassels
Needle
Off-white thread
Straight pins

Tools
Rotary cutter
Cutting mat
16½-inch-square clear acrylic ruler
Sewing gauge
Iron and ironing board
Scissors
Sewing machine

Note: This valance was designed for a 36-inch-wide window. Adjust the number or size of the squares as desired for your window opening.

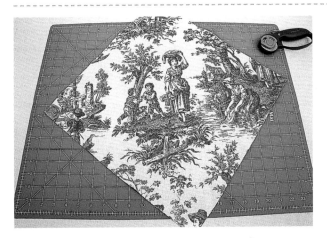

1. With the rotary cutter and ruler, cut five 16½-inch squares of toile, making sure that the pattern is centered and on point.

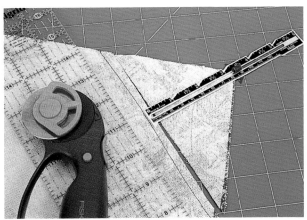

2. Sew the first two squares together, right sides facing, approximately 3 inches from one side corner. Trim off the excess fabric, leaving a ¼-inch seam. Open the squares and seam the next square to the center square, right sides facing, 3 inches from the opposite corner; trim the seam. Continue in this manner to seam the remaining squares to form a chain of five squares total. Overcast stitch along the seam edges.

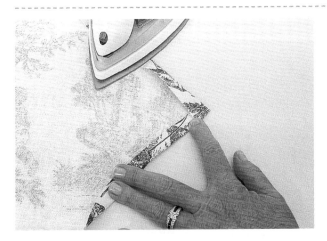

3. Fold all of the raw edges under ½ inch to the wrong side and press. (If needed, open the seams slightly at the ends so that the folds lay flat.) Sew trim along the folded edges (see "Applying Trims," page 34). Stitch tassels to the bottom corner of each square.

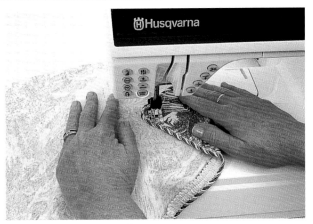

4. For the casing, fold each top corner over approximately 3 inches to the wrong side and pin in place. Straight stitch along the folded points to secure the casing.

bandanna valance

Bandannas make great, inexpensive window treatments that have that easy-going, no-fuss air adored by both young and old alike. Leave the valance edge plain or add a frilly trim for extra length and color.

SKILL LEVEL Beginner

FINISHED SIZE
84- by 24-inch valance

WHAT YOU'LL NEED

Fabric
4 denim paisley bandannas
Four 21½-inch-square white
    bandannas
Blue thread
Sewing needle
Straight pins

Supplies
2½ yards of white 2-inch ruffle trim

Tools
Rotary cutter
Cutting mat
24½-inch clear acrylic ruler
Sewing gauge
Iron and ironing board
Seam opener
Scissors
Sewing machine

Note: This valance was designed for a 36-inch-wide window. Adjust the number or size of the bandannas as desired to fit your window opening.

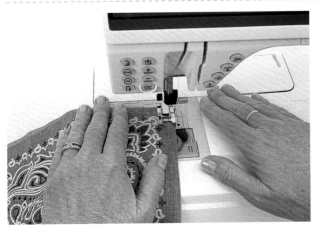

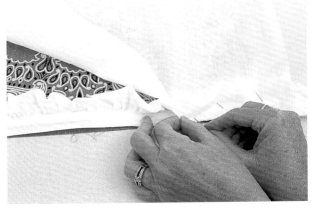

1. Using the decorative borders as a guide, cut off the plain outer edges of the denim paisley bandanna approximately ¾ inch from each edge. Cut the white bandannas into squares the same size as the denim paisley; press. With right sides facing, using a ¼-inch seam allowance, sew the denim bandannas together to form a long rectangle. Repeat to seam the white bandannas together. Press the seams open.

2. On the right side, pin trim along the bottom edge of the denim rectangle. Layer the white rectangle over the denim, right sides facing, sandwiching the trim in between (see "Applying Trims," page 34). Sew the layers together with a ¼-inch seam, leaving a 5-inch opening on one end. Turn right side out, press, and whipstitch the end closed (see "Stitch Glossary," page 33).

3. To sew a 1¼-inch casing, using a sewing gauge as a guide, sew two rows of straight stitching 2¼ inches and 3½ inches from the top edge. (Note: The casing is designed to fit a ¾-inch-wide curtain rod. Allow more or less space for larger or smaller rods, as needed.)

4. Using the seam opener, open the ends of the casing and slip the curtain onto the rod.

tied valance

Tie the ends of fabric squares onto a curtain rod for a quick and easy window treatment. When tying the squares to the rod, remember to tie the knots in the same direction. Combine prints and colors for a lively appearance.

SKILL LEVEL Beginner

FINISHED SIZE
Ten 16-inch squares

WHAT YOU'LL NEED

Fabric
½ yard each of pink print, blue print, pink/blue stripes, and pink/blue print

Supplies
Blue thread

Tools
Rotary cutter
Cutting mat
16½-inch-square clear acrylic ruler
Iron and ironing board
Scissors
Sewing machine

Note: This valance was designed for a 24-inch-wide window. Adjust the number or size of the squares as desired to fit your window opening.

1. With the rotary cutter and ruler, cut two 16½-inch squares from each fabric.

2. Fold all of the raw edges under ¼ inch to the wrong side and press the folds flat.

3. Sew an overcast stitch along all of the raw edges (see "Stitch Glossary," page 32).

4. Tie one end of each square on point onto the curtain rod, as shown, alternating fabrics and keeping the squares evenly spaced along the rod.

suppliers

Listed are the manufacturers of and suppliers for many of the materials used in this book. Most of these companies sell their products exclusively to fabric and craft retailers, which are a consumer's most dependable sources for sewing supplies. Your local retailer can advise you on purchases, and if you need something they don't have in stock, they will usually order it for you. If you can't find a store in your area that carries a particular item or will accept a request for an order, or if you need special assistance, a manufacturer will direct you to the retailer nearest you that carries their products and will try to answer any technical questions you might have.

Beacon Adhesives Inc.
125 MacQuesten Parkway South
Mount Vernon, NY 10550-1779
914-699-3400
www.beacon1.com
Glue

Carolina Manufacturing
P.O. Box 9138
7025 Augusta Rd.
Greenville, SC 29605
www.carolinamfg.com
Bandannas

Coats & Clark
P.O. Box 12229
Greenville, SC 29612-0229
800-648-1479
www.coatsandclark.com
Thread and Embroidery Floss

Daisy Kingdom
P.O. Box 10232
Rock Hill, SC 29731
1-800-234-6688
www.daisykingdom.com.
Fabric

Fiskars®, Inc.
7811 West Stewart Ave.
Wausau, WI 54402-8027
www.fiskars.com
Cutting Tools, Rulers, and Mats

JewelCraft LLC
505 Winsor Drive
Secaucus, NJ 07094
201-223-0804
www.jewelcraft.biz
Trims & Beads

Poly-fil® by Fairfield Processing
P.O. Box 1130
Danbury, CT 06813-1130
800-980-8000
www.poly-fil.com
Batting, Pillow Forms and Poly-fil

Prym-Dritz USA
P.O. Box 5028
Spartanburg, SC 29304
www.dritz.com
Trims, Mats, and Rulers

St. Louis Trimming, Division of TrimTex Company, Inc.
400 Park Ave.
Williamsport, PA 17701
570-326-9135
Trims

Therm-O-Web
770 Glenn Avenue
Wheeling, IL 60090
847-520-5200
www.thermoweb.com
Iron-on Adhesives

Viking Sewing Machine, Inc.
31000 Viking Parkway
Westlake, OH 44145
www.husqvarnaviking.com
Sewing Machines

Waverly
F. Schumacher & Co.
79 Madison Avenue
New York, NY 10016
800-423-5881
www.waverly.com
Fabric

Wrights®
85 South St.
P.O. Box 398
West Warren, MA 01092
1-877-597-4448
www.wrights.com
Trims

Getting in Touch

Kathy Peterson
www.kathypeterson.com

Christopher Lincoln Photography
1-800-221-5402
CLPhotography@aol.com

index

About the Author

The work of designer Kathy Peterson has been published in numerous craft and women's magazines and has been featured on several nationally broadcast television shows, including *The Christopher Lowell Show, Home Matters* (both on the Discovery Channel), *The Carol Duvall Show, Decorating with Style, Today at Home* (on HGTV and DIY), *Aleene's Creative Living,* and *Your Home Studio* (on TNN). Kathy is also the host of her own national TV show *Town & Country Crafts with Kathy Peterson* (on GoodLife TV and The Family Net) and is the author of several craft books. She lives in Tequesta, Florida.

About the Photographer

Christopher Lincoln is a commercial photographer and graphic illustrator whose company, Lincoln Productions, is based in Jupiter, Florida.